T0027094

Praise for Michelle de Kretser

"I so admire Michelle de Kretser's formidable technique—her characters feel alive, and she can create a sweeping narrative that encompasses years and yet still retain the sharp, almost hallucinatory detail."   —HILARY MANTEL

"It is impossible to describe de Kretser's prose as anything but rich, luxuriant, intense, and gorgeous."
—ANITA DESAI

"De Kretser's displaced and subtle characters are genuinely interesting, and her writing is emotionally accurate."   —URSULA K. LE GUIN

"Michelle de Krester knows how to construct a gripping story. She writes quickly and lightly of wonderful and terrible things . . . A master storyteller."   —A. S. BYATT

"Novel by novel, the Sri Lankan–born Australian has emerged as one of the most fiercely intelligent voices in fiction today."

—BOYD TONKIN, *The Independent*

On Shirley Hazzard

On **Shirley Hazzard**

Michelle de Kretser

Catapult
New York

Originally published in Australia by Black Inc. in
association with the University of Melbourne and
State Library Victoria.

Grateful acknowledgment is made to the
following for permission to reprint material:

"A Spark of Laurel" copyright © 1958 by Stanley
Kunitz, from *The Collected Poems* by Stanley Kunitz.
Used by permission of W. W. Norton & Company, Inc.

"A Map of Verona" by Henry Reed, 1942. Used by
permission of the Royal Literary Fund.

ISBN: 978-1-948226-82-0

Jacket design by Sarah Brody
Book design by Wah-Ming Chang

Catapult titles are distributed to the trade by
Publishers Group West
Phone: 866-400-5351

Library of Congress Control Number: 2019944450

Printed in the United States of America
10 9 8 7 6 5 4 3 2 1

For **Sarah Lutyens**

Works of art can be more important than anything critics can say about them.

SHIRLEY HAZZARD,
"We Need Silence to Find
Out What We Think"

I've carried in my head
For twenty years and more
Some lines you wrote

—STANLEY KUNITZ,
"A Spark of Laurel"

On Shirley Hazzard

An Ending

In December 2016 an email came to tell me that Shirley Hazzard had died. I read it and began to cry. It was a response to the crushing *Too late!* that attends all our negotiations with the dead. I was a reader weeping because now there would be no more books; I was a writer weeping because now I could never write to Hazzard, telling her what her work meant to me and thanking her for it.

The tears went on, returning steadily, stealthily as day followed day. This silent, unstoppable cascade embarrassed me. It felt excessive. Hazzard was eighty-five. I knew that she'd been ill for some years, latterly spending the greater portion of her days asleep. She had been well cared for during her decline. I'd never met her, never corresponded with her—I could argue no personal tie. Mutual friends seemed largely undisturbed by her death; it was, as they pointed out gently, a good ending and not unexpected. My weeping felt imposterish, as if I were claiming a connection that didn't exist.

At some point in those sorrowful days there came into my mind Jacob Burckhardt's declaration, quoted by Hazzard, that Italy belonged to all who fell under its spell "by right of admiration." So, fittingly, it was Hazzard herself who provided the explanation for my tears: they flowed by right of admiration.

How to Account for It?

Hazzard was the first Australian writer I read who looked outwards, away from Australia. Her work spoke of places from which I had come and places to which I longed to go. It conjured cities and rooms: sociable spaces. Yet what she had to say was expansive, not enclosed—I felt enlarged by it, my view widened. It was reading as an affair of revelations and gifts. It fell like rain, greening my vision of Australian literature as a stony country where I would never feel at home. Splendor had entered the scene.

She describes a fresco: "The impression it made was unaccountable; there was nothing in any of its details to suggest the splendour of the whole."

Faced with writing about her work, I ask myself: how to account for the impression of splendor?

It's striking how frequently Hazzard evokes the value of phenomena that resist description. She notes the "incommunicable grandeur" of a landscape, and the "silent, inestimable losses" that modernity brings. It's hardly unusual for a writer to appreciate the expert articulation of experience, but it's rarer to find one who prizes what expertise can't say. "Unaccountable" is a word that recurs when Hazzard writes about literature or painting. It acknowledges the mystery that resides in art, as well as the contingent nature of our response. A book comes to find you at a particular season of your life. Afterwards, nothing is the same.

I decide to quote Hazzard extensively in this essay. I repeat my mantra: literature lives in

sentences. Quotation seems the best way of indi-
cating what I admire in Hazzard as well as giving
readers unmediated access to her prose.

As soon as I begin, I'm beset by doubt. I have
the impression that I've been entrusted with
something large and shimmering and whole, and
that in attempting to hand it on, I'm reducing it
to shards. Instead of conveying the moonlight, all
I'm showing is the glitter of broken glass.

Julian Barnes cites Degas: "Do you think you
can explain the merits of a picture to those who
do not see them? . . . Among people who under-
stand, words are not necessary, you say, *humph,
he, ha*, and everything has been said."

Humph, he, ha.

STRAYA

One reason for the affinity I feel with Hazzard is the question mark that hovers over our right to be considered Australian: in her case, because she left the country at the age of sixteen; in mine, because I didn't arrive until I was fourteen.

Hazzard, born in 1931, described the Australia in which she grew up as "a country where sameness was a central virtue." It was "a remote, philistine country in those years, and very much a male country, dominated by a defiant masculinity that repudiated the arts."

Others of Hazzard's generation have said the same thing. And with Hazzard, there was the additional factor of her youth; her experience of Australia was necessarily limited, confined to the circles of home and school. Children mistake their families for the world—how can they do anything else?

Yet, from a passage in *The Transit of Venus* describing the Bell sisters' childhood in Sydney: "Once in a while, or all the time, there was the sense of something supreme and obvious waiting to be announced."

In middle age, Caroline Bell expresses a wish to return to Australia to see what she was "incapable of seeing as a child."

In *The Transit of Venus*—that great narrative of observation—an "antipodean" way of seeing is described as "a clear perception unmingled with suspiciousness." Antipodean seeing is radical, interrupting "the smooth flow of acceptance." It draws attention to what has been normalized and rendered invisible. Caro sees a heavy wardrobe in a room and thinks of the men who had to carry it up the stairs. Her insight is connected to the antipodean origins that make her an outsider in England; excluded from power, she can see how it works.

"Antipodean," a term often used patronizingly in the northern hemisphere, is recouped here by Hazzard. Through spending time with Caro, Ted begins to see as she does. Antipodean seeing is accurate: a compliment smuggled into the most Australian of Hazzard's books.

Down the years, whenever I've mentioned my admiration of Hazzard, there has always been someone—no, let me be accurate: there has always been an older man who wields intellectual and cultural power—to inform me that I'm quite wrong. Her Boyer Lectures of 1984, published as *Coming of Age in Australia*, are raised. Am I familiar with them? I admit that I'm not. Thereupon I'm assured that if only I knew Hazzard's views on Australia, I would go over at once to Camp Contempt.

Coming of Age in Australia is held in any well-stocked library, but it remained the one work of Hazzard's that I hadn't read. I was afraid of what it would reveal: condescension, ignorance, snobbery, at best a glib dismissiveness—all these things had been implied or said. My editor, learning that I didn't have a copy, kindly sent me his own. My reluctance to read the thing can be gauged from the promptness with which I lost it. The book had to be somewhere in my study, but although I searched and searched, I couldn't find it. At last, after many tactical delays—it was too hot or too rainy or I was far too busy to go to the library—I borrowed a copy. When I couldn't postpone the ordeal any longer, I opened the book and began to read gingerly, mentally peeping through fingers over eyes.

Hazzard depicts the Australia of her childhood, and the "great transformations" that had come by 1984. She opens modestly, referring to her "brief formal education," describing herself as "an ignorant person." She offers impressions of contemporary Australia that are generous and optimistic. I imagine her anticipating hostility to her criticisms and taking pains to make it clear that she sees the best in us, too. It's a courteous approach. At the same time, it chafes. Would a man feel obliged to lead in like that? Even today, a woman writing in forthright, personal ways can feel it necessary to signal harmlessness at the outset. Maggie Nelson is about as different a writer from Hazzard as can be imagined, yet *The Argonauts* opens with a staging of physical and emotional vulnerability. The subtext in both cases is the same: "I am not a threat."

Hazzard goes on to caution against nationalism and propose a vision of what the nation might yet be: cosmopolitan, kind, "living without an enemy." She hopes for an Australian future that is open to the past, including "the prehistoric existence of Aboriginal peoples on this continent," as well as to the world: to "the vast, diverse civilisation carried here by two centuries of new settlers."

But Hazzard doesn't flatter, and that stung. "Australia is not an innocent country. This nation's short recorded history is shadowed, into the present day, by the fate of its native peoples, by forms of unyielding prejudice, by a strain of derision and unexamined violence, and by a persistent current of misogyny." These criticisms, commonplace today, were considerably less so then. In 1984, in the wake of winning the America's Cup and the lead-up to the Bicentenary, Australia was in the grip of an ebullient—shading into bullish—nationalism, the flipside of our chronic insecurity about our standing in the world. Into that climate, Hazzard delivered lectures that called the nation to account: among other things, for a whiny tendency to look on ourselves as beleaguered victims when we are among the luckiest people on earth. Patrick White, too, had deplored the smallness of our big country, ramping up criticism with his trademark ferocity. But Hazzard had lived most of her life outside Australia, which from a nationalist perspective disqualified her from offering any opinion about the country that wasn't wholly complimentary. Perhaps she thought that the merciless dissection of English social snobbery and American political arrogance in her work licensed her to call it as she saw it in regard to Australia. But that's not how it plays.

Another thing—possibly the decisive factor: Hazzard's tone throughout the lectures is lucidly trenchant. It's enough for a woman to *take that tone* to get up the noses of certain men.

Shamefully, I had believed the men. The men were intelligent, credentialed, and articulate. Those are explanations but there's no excuse. I had failed to abide by the reader's first principle: read it for yourself.

It's my strong hope that everyone reading this will go on to read Hazzard for themselves.

RESPONSES TO READING

For Hazzard, understanding a work of literature requires "a submission akin to that of generosity or love." It's a sentiment that echoes Susan Sontag's call for an erotics of interpretation: for attentiveness to the experience on offer, rather than a concern with analysis that can quickly glide into fantasies of superiority. The ecstatic yielding of the self, while not canceling out assessment, seeks to illuminate rather than usurp the work in question.

"In responsive reading, one participates, so to speak, in the rainbow of creation," writes Hazzard. Where receptiveness is present, it "evokes an individual response rather than the authorised one." The work can "reach into the reader's soul."

Gioconda, in *The Bay of Noon*, describes her visit to an art gallery: "They had a notice, *Please do not touch the paintings*; they should forbid the paintings to touch you."

Hazzard had an unwavering belief in the power of art to transform, comfort, reveal. She said that at a time of great personal unhappiness, poetry had saved her life. She grew up in an age when poetry cut across generation and class. "One never knew where it would turn up. Like mercy." It was "in books that one discovered affinity, event, extension."

In *The Great Fire*, Helen and Benedict have been "delivered" from the pettiness of their parents by literature. As a fifteen-year-old schoolgirl,

Hazzard bought an expensive book of essays, "smuggling it home to avoid trouble," about the "flourish of independence" her action represented. The book brought "an ecstasy of reading that dazzled the eyes."

"When I was fifteen, sixteen, I had already lived deeply in poetry." The sensations aroused by poems were "private, intuitive, unaccountable." Hardy's poems about his dead wife, which Hazzard discovered when she was young and in love, were "transcendent": "I ate and drank them up as nourishment, knowing they could only do me good." At seventeen, she read Leopardi in translation and began learning Italian in order to read him in the original.

Hazzard's formal education ended at sixteen; after that, she simply went on reading everything. With no sense of incongruity, she could describe Proust as "a late love" because she was over twenty when she read him for the first time.

———

In a story in *Cliffs of Fall*, a character believes that practical considerations can be overturned "by a single line of poetry." Poetry is the equivalent here of "human": a favorite Hazzard adjective, used in contradistinction to whatever, in the name of reason or progress, seeks to grind down the soul.

But there's nothing sentimental or fuzzy about Hazzard's veneration of poetry. She quotes Flaubert: "Poetry is as precise as geometry." And John Bayley, on "the inevitable solace that right language brings." Right language for Hazzard was exact language: the finding of the accurate word.

When *We Need Silence to Find Out What We Think*, a collection of Hazzard's essays, was published, a reader told me in a tone of amused disdain, "She likes Tennyson!" In fact, if quotation is proof of partiality, the essays show that Hazzard also liked Horace, Petrarch, Whitman, Baudelaire,

Coleridge, Parra, Stevens, Miłosz, Byron, Homer, Yeats ... as well as Montale, Leopardi, and Auden, the last three quoted repeatedly and at length. But it was Tennyson, disparaged by T. S. Eliot in his empire-building phase and dismissed by the sheeplike ever since, who was singled out in the belief that to quote him showed preposterous judgment. Not that Hazzard would have cared: she possessed the autodidact's independence of taste.

She had a prodigious memory and could recite long poems by heart. "Where there was greatness, the words seemed inevitable, as if memory had been awaiting them." Her friendship with Graham Greene originated with poetry. At their first meeting Hazzard supplied a line by Browning that Greene was trying and failing to recall. The incident struck her like a meeting in a novel: "a real novel, a good novel, an old novel."

———

"If you learned the stuff young you never lost it." That Christian, in *The Transit of Venus*, refers to poetry as "stuff" is revealing. So are the poems he remembers: well-worn anthology staples. He knows no others—and it's his failure to look beyond the authorized that Hazzard treats ironically rather than the putative merits of the poems themselves. Or perhaps that's what I want to believe: I learned them young, too, those poems that are rarely encountered these days. Reading *The Transit of Venus*, I came to the place where Christian remembers a line by Southey and found myself falling through a hole twenty years deep. With no warning I was aged nine, in a classroom beside the Indian Ocean. *Oh Christ! It is the Inchcape Rock!*

There are works that pass from literature into autobiography. Then questions of worth are beside the point.

She likes Tennyson.
Onya, Shirl!

LIKE COLOR IN A PAINTING

L earn the stuff young and it sharpens the ear. Hazzard read her work aloud to her self to get the rhythms right. The movement of poetry infiltrates her prose. It lends liveliness to print: music rises from the page.

She often ends a sentence with a stressed monosyllable. "The decline of a sea-girt house offers no phase of seedy charm." The effect is not simply of closing a door, but of shooting the bolt home. The sentence is sealed.

Along with music, what might a novelist take from poetry? I think Hazzard took precision, swiftness, a taste for compression.

Tancredi, in *The Evening of the Holiday*, has "the qualities that are attractive about Italy itself—grace and the lack of earnestness." In *The Bay of Noon*, Neapolitan speech is "splendid": "single words forming entire narrations, phrases deployed like colour in a painting." These things could equally be said of Hazzard's prose. She was a writer who honored the sentence. Unusually for a novelist, she wrote memorable ones. She saw the connection between good writing and truth—that literature happens where the surprising word or the unexpected figure is also the most accurate: "It is a recurring error of criticism . . . to treat 'style' as an insubstantial literary contrivance distinct from the author's so-called 'material.'"

Hazzard writes of soldiers squirming in "the ill-fitting clutch" of their uniforms. Of the "mad grin" of lightning, and of the sound of a bell "widening" into a room. She describes hair "tinselled" by sea air.

(Like Conrad, whom she read and reread, Hazzard always writes well of the sea. After all, she grew up looking at Sydney Harbour.)

———

Language is examined up close in Hazzard's work. "We are human beings, not rational ones." The stock phrase "human beings" is disrupted by isolating its first element; the mind receives a little jolt.

The pressing of dead figures of speech into life is particularly marked in *The Transit of Venus*. A female character railing against assigned gender roles says, "Women have got to fight their way out of that dumb waiting at the end of the never-ringing telephone. The *receiver*, as our portion of it is called."

Elsewhere the strategy serves satire: "Christian Thrale was now rising in his profession. Those peering into the oven of his career would report, 'Christian is rising,' as if he were a cake or a loaf of bread."

Words that recur in Hazzard's writing: "human," "mercy," "revelation."

LESSONS IN ADJECTIVES

The "incisive fronds" of a laurel.

A "furled poplar."

An "administrative smile."

A father's "hard, omnipotent arms."

"The floral English summer."

"A bathroom varicose with streaked marble."

An "immoderate sunset."

An "infirm chair" in a room of "unconvinced Westernism."

"His first engagement with lion grief."

"Asia's unapologetic smells."

Old buildings whose "violated and ghostly elegance" persists.

Places

There were days in winter when the narrow spiralling streets of this town were reduced to slippery channels banked with snow; when, viewed from the foot of its hill, the city rose up like a symmetrical, frosted fir tree, branching into great terraces of church, palace, and piazza."

"Ordinariness, the affliction and backbone of other cities, was here nonexistent. Phrases I had always thought universal—the common people, the average family, the typical reaction, ordinary life—had no meaning where people were all uncommon and life extraordinary."

"Tancredi had grown up in Sicily, where no entertaining is ever done in the summer afternoons, where there is a solitary, almost therapeutic drinking of lemonade or almond milk in darkened rooms before the sun goes down."

"A town of overhead wires and small discouraged shops."

"Brick houses were symmetric with red, yellow, or purple respectability: low garden walls, wide verandas, recurrent clumps of frangipani and hibiscus, of banksia and bottlebrush; perhaps a summerhouse, perhaps a flagpole. Never a sign of washing or even of people: such evidence must be sought inside, or at the back."

"A weatherboard town with telegraph poles and the sort of picture-house where you could hear the rain."

"Filth was in fact on Peter Exley's mind in those first weeks: the accretion filming the Orient, the shimmer of sweat or excrement. A railing or handle one's fingers would not willingly grasp; walls and objects grimed with existence; the limp, soiled, colonial money, little notes curled and withered, like shavings from some discarded central lode."

"From intersections you could see, beyond the quays, the blue harbour and far mountains, whose incommunicable grandeur might, for all the town seemed to care, have hung there on a calendar."

Hazzard's fiction depicts young women traveling to new places and reckoning with strangeness. Her first two novels also end with journeys, wonderfully described. The narratives are open-ended, the women at their center moving out towards change.

The Transit of Venus, too, ends with a journey, but here the narrative is tragic, end-stopped. Travel is perilous in Hazzard's fiction. An astounding number of planes crash over the course of her work; a ferry capsizes, ships are sunk, a man dies because a boat's engine fails. My guess is that somewhere in her mind Hazzard associated travel with the Second World War—hence with danger. In *The Bay of Noon*, Jenny remembers the names of ships destroyed during the war; the list is impressive. Like Jenny, Hazzard was a child during that war, which she likens to "a great syphon that sprayed human beings all over the globe."

Hazzard left Australia in 1947. The journey brought marvels; also appalling knowledge. One of the ports at which the ship called was Hiroshima. Hazzard was sixteen; it was barely two years after the city's destruction. Unsurprisingly, the encounter is branded into her fiction. Hiroshima was a place where "the merciful were at an even worse disadvantage than usual."

POLITICS

One of Caro's female co-workers in *The Transit of Venus* says, "You feel down-right disloyal to your experience, when you do come across a man you could like. By then you scarcely see how you can decently make terms, it's like going over to the enemy."

The narrator continues: "All this was indis putable, even brave. But was a map, from which rooms, hours, and human faces did not rise; on which there was no bloom of generosity or discovery. The omissions might constitute life itself."

A map is a metaphor for faith: an agreed-on simplification of complexity. In two different books, Hazzard quotes Henry Reed's poem about the inadequacy of maps:

Maps are of place, not time, nor can they say
The surprising height and colour of a building
Nor where the groups of people bar the way.

Novels, unlike maps, are a form of counter-point; they exist to create fruitful complications. (Karl Kraus defined a writer as someone who makes a riddle out of an answer.) Novelists' minds tilt to exceptions; to the omissions that might constitute life. "Singularity engaged him": Hazzard's remark about Graham Greene applies equally to herself. No wonder, since novelists trade in a form that fetishizes the individual—which is to say, ambiguity and contradiction, "all the movement of meaning which we know to be the nature of life."

Politics, on the other hand, requires maps. Political life is grounded in solidarity and belief. Brigitta Olubas writes that Hazzard's politics are "consistently of the Left." But Hazzard remains wary of the political in the sense of formal affiliations. As a character in *The Transit of Venus* observes, "Even a right side imposes wrongful silences, required untruths."

That kind of thing tends not to please anyone. But Hazzard was concerned with truth, not with finding favor. "Nothing creates such untruth in you as the wish to please."

Hazzard reserves solidarity for the vulnerable— for whoever is oppressed, disregarded, or outcast rather than for a specific cause. The victims of a Latin American dictator, the survivors of Hiroshima, colonized people, workers of all kinds, the poor, the socially inept, rejected lovers, war veterans, foreigners, stray animals, or simply the targets of ordinary, workaday malice: all engage her sympathetic attention.

She practices an ethics of noticing. Charlotte Wood, writing about *The Transit of Venus*, paraphrases Iris Murdoch: "Paying attention is a moral act."

———

From *The Transit of Venus*:

> My window looks on a courtyard full
> of flowering trees—hawthorn, a Judas
> tree, and, very near, a big lilac coming
> out in purple pyramids. There is a foun-
> tain and—concealed—a thrush. During
> the holiday I drove with two French col-
> leagues to the mines near Lille, where we
> went down a pit. The coal-face straight
> from Dante, worked by boys of sixteen
> or so, mostly North Africans who spoke
> no French. Worse than this were the hov-
> els they went back to afterwards, ten to a
> filthy hut.

If there had been a paragraph break after
"thrush," the first two sentences would have been
skillful scene-setting. Without the break, the primary function of those sentences is to point up an
obscenity; they make the shocking information
that follows more shocking. It's a lesson in how

the arrangement of sentences can speak political truth.

Where Hazzard's politics show unequivocally is in her refusal to be cowed by power—her scorn for it, in fact. Her two nonfiction books about the United Nations, *Defeat of an Ideal* and *Countenance of Truth*, are political in the conventional sense. The first documents the history of U.S. intervention in the organization and the consequent mutilation of its aims. The second details a story Hazzard had broken in a piece of investigative reporting, Secretary-General Kurt Waldheim's cover-up of his Nazi past.

Here are two passages from *The Transit of Venus* that are concerned with war. They're quiet, incidental passages (one of them is literally parenthetical), told from the perspective of minor characters. A less confident writer would have made much more of them. Hazzard knew that quietness is a force.

(In 1916, during the Battle of the Somme, Charmian Playfair, volunteering as a nurse's aide, was assigned to ambulance duty at Victoria Station where casualties were arriving on hospital trains. The loaded ambulance trundled back through dark streets carrying its racks of blanketed men—who, from their spotless newspaper anonymity of "the wounded," were suddenly incarnate as moaning, silent, or plucky inhabitants of rent, individual flesh. Enclosed with these spectres in swaying gloom, a nineteen-year-old girl put her hand to her soft throat. Yet moved as best she could, to supply water or answer questions, among the grey blankets and the red, rusty, or blackened bandages. There was a boy of her own age to whose whisper she had to bend, her face nearly touching his: "So cold. Cold. My feet are so cold." And, almost capably, the girl answered, "I'll fix that"; turning to adjust the blanket, and discovering he had no feet.)

Someone came to the open window and threw a cigarette accurately into a dark pond in the garden. There was the flicker, the sizzle, and a small protest from insects or a frog.

The old physicist stood by the window, hitching his belt. Recalling a night of war when he had done fire-watching on the roof of the Savoy. The black river reflected, red and white, the flames and searchlights, the earth rocked and shuddered with the impact and recoil of armoury. And a burning plane twirled down from the sky, shedding its pilot, who plunged in his separate fire. The plane exploded in fragments before reaching earth, but the blazing man plummeted to the river, which—as if he had been a cigarette butt—sizzled him out forever.

Both passages derive their force largely from their calm accounting of the price that bodies pay in war. But that isn't the only source of their power. In the first extract, there's the girl's stunned realization, shared by the reader, that nothing can "fix" what has happened.

The second passage deals graphically with war, witnessing, violent death. The burning pilot is one of those Hazzard images that remain imprinted on the inner eye long after the end of the book. But the narration of those large, horrific things, which could so easily have spun out into windy abstraction, is earthed by the specificity of a detail everyone has, at some time, observed: an old man hitching his belt. Trust is created: efficiently, without show.

WEAPONS

A character in *People in Glass Houses* is "humorous, compassionate and incorruptible—these invaluable qualities being listed here by order of importance." Hazzard never makes the mistake of conflating humor with triviality: she is very serious and very funny. Not nearly enough has been made of the comedic brilliance of her work.

She writes that art offers "immemorial immediacy"; it nurtures a "directness to life." By contrast, official life is "remote from life itself." The gap between people and situations as they are—grandiose, vicious, deluded, foolish, self-congratulatory—and as they could be is where Hazzard inserts her wit.

Irony and satire are her preferred weapons, as they are those of Christina Stead and Patrick White. They're antipodean weapons, the weapons of the outsider; a way of seeing that punctures and deflates.

"They were well-educated, pious women, and much of their conversation was taken up with illustrating the fundamental worth of human nature—a quality not always susceptible of illustration and, when illustrated, not always interesting."

"Not naturally malicious, he had developed rapidly since entering bureaucracy."

"He was, for so industrious a man, remarkably able."

"Swoboda was not a brilliant man. He was a man of what used to be known as average and is now known as above-average intelligence."

"Gianni ground the pepper mill as if wringing someone's neck."

"He found these women uncommonly self-possessed for their situation. They seemed scarcely conscious of being Australians in a furnished flat."

"Britain had shared its squalor readily enough with far Australia, though withholding the Abbey and the Swan of Avon."

"There were papers marked PUS, for the Permanent Under-Secretary of State."

"There was a century here of obscure imperial dejection: a room of listless fevers. Of cafard, ennui and other French diseases. The encrusted underside of glory."

"Audacity had been exhausted in arriving at the uttermost point of the earth. They wished above all to pretend that nothing had happened."

THE EVENING OF THE HOLIDAY

Hazzard had the courage to take love seriously in her fiction: to write about it intelligently, respectfully, and without flinching. Courage is required because when a woman writes about love, the result—however faceted and splendid—risks being branded lite. In Australia, a reviewer described *The Transit of Venus* as "the best-dressed women's magazine fiction of its year." I think of it every time I see his byline: pinned to him forever, his badge of shame.

In *The Evening of the Holiday* and *Cliffs of Fall*, love is offered "without reserve," usually by young women who have yet to realize that it's a "subtle game." It's a youthful way of looking at love, one that would be easy to mock, but Hazzard refuses to treat it ironically; forty years later, it remains Helen's way of loving in *The Great Fire*. It leaves the one who loves unprotected, and Hazzard's sympathy always flies to the vulnerable. To repudiate that way of loving—openly, without defenses—and approach love coolly instead is like "following the score instead of listening to the music."

I admire Hazzard for valuing the intensity of emotional truth, for refusing to sneer. But Sophie in *The Evening of the Holiday* and her counterparts in *Cliffs of Fall* are suspended in love like specimens in fluid. Loving a man selflessly is these women's luminous fixation—they have no other. It maroons them in time. They are strange. Their world is both recognizably ours and remote. They inhabit a plot about female subjectivity that has withered on the vine. Their strangeness, the strangeness of realism outrun by reality, disturbs.

Helen, from *The Great Fire*, is different; like Hazzard's colonial officials, she has a period air. She isn't strange but quaint. We—writer and readers alike—look at her across the safe, constructed distance of historical fiction. Helen is also very young, and love doesn't keep her from the proper, serious business of the young, which is education.

Jenny in *The Bay of Noon* and Caro in *The Transit of Venus* belong to modernity. They love passionately and suffer for it, but not to the exclusion of everything else.

In *The Evening of the Holiday*, published in 1966, we are told that Tancredi "liked the idea of supremacy and believed, correctly, that women want to be prevailed upon." Four years later came *The Bay of Noon*. In that novel, when Gianni tries to kiss Jenny on an outing, she refuses to be "prevailed upon." Correctly has become mistakenly. Feminism has happened. Adverbs have changed.

———

Yet *The Evening of the Holiday* contains very great passages. Sophie and Tancredi's visit to the farmhouse on his property is one. In the presence of the tenant farmers, Sophie sees Tancredi in a new role. "His authority, their humility, made her uneasy." Tancredi is revealed as "the beneficiary of privilege so all-pervasive that it could not even be described as entrenched." Previously, the lovers have been sufficient unto themselves; their passion has enclosed them in a sphere. Now that sphere is penetrated by knowledge: of class relations, work, poverty, the misery ingrained in social history.

Sophie's hands, resting on the table, are white and soft, the nails painted, one wrist encircled by a bracelet. They contrast with the hands of the farmers, roughened and darkened by labor. The description revises an early scene in which Sophie's hand, plunging into a fountain to retrieve that same bracelet, signals the moment when Tancredi is first drawn to her. In the farmhouse, that soft, manicured hand is no longer an eroticized fetish but a marker of privilege.

When Sophie looks at the face of the Virgin in a barely there fresco in the barn, she sees "some utter forgetfulness, some monumental knowledge never imparted and now irretrievably mislaid." She leaves the farm, however, with new understanding. The episode ends with the lovers returned to their private world: "There were just the solitary trees, the lake of grasses and red flowers, and two figures descending the upward path." But the end of love has begun.

In the novel's closing pages, Sophie, having arrived too late to say goodbye to her dying aunt, decides not to stay on for the funeral. The entire episode is magnificent: the description of grief and of the mourners, of the moment when Sophie, visiting the town for the last time, sees Tancredi's parked car. Then she's in the train, which is full of soldiers—who, judging by their youth and inexperience, appear to be discharging their compulsory military service. At each station, one of them begins a tune on his bugle; when the train starts up again, the instrument shakes and the music breaks off. "But after each such departure, for a little while, the bugler tried to keep playing, to reach the end of the song; and these last notes, wobbling and swaying, persisted out of the station and into the countryside until the train, gathering speed, made it impossible to play any longer."

At first, the cadence of that final sentence follows the bugler's music: the clauses separated by commas enact the effort involved and the jerkiness of the melody, while the disruption brought about by the semicolon reflects the broken tune. Then the rhythm moves from the wobble and sway of the bugle to mimicking the sound of the train, its gathering speed as it rushes away. It's a beautifully composed sentence, and it points to the effect of modernity on an "antiquated sentimental tune."

It's no accident that the strongest scenes in the novel involve interruption and endings.

Knowledge of violence—embedded in class structures, embodied in the soldiers—is making itself felt. History is assuming the upper hand in Hazzard's work.

Place is dominant in *The Evening of the Holiday*. Afterwards, all the novels will be about people and places in time.

Lessons in

Characterization

He and Evie had been very happy together for fifteen years. Long ago, however, at his own expense and to everyone's surprise, he had published a small book of love poems that carried no assurance of being addressed to her."

"He would never ask himself 'What will become of me?'—much less the more terrifying question 'What has become of me?'"

A man speaks loudly "in order not to be afraid, like a person in the dark."

"Graham's humour had a keen edge: the snowball that conceals the stone."

"When these girls were small their parents had drowned in a capsized ferry. Christian was to refer to this as 'a boating accident' for the rest of his life."

"He had the complexion, lightly webbed, of outdoor living and indoor drinking."

"Dora sat on a corner of the spread rug, longing to be assigned some task so she could resent it."

"Rysom was forever doing imitations: of a language, an accent, a personality; a man."

"Judging him a poor thing, she would yet have married him and given him a devoted form of hell."

"Too cautious to detest, Mrs. Baillie did, with some regularity, not quite like."

PEOPLE IN GLASS HOUSES

Graham Greene observed that "in child-hood, all books are books of divination, telling us about the future." When I was young I read novels that described friendship, love, sorrow, politics, the drama of family, the lives of women, intellectual and creative endeavor—novels that were preludes to the adventure of life. The knowledge they offered was dreamlike: not a matter of blueprints but of colors and impressions. Yet it illuminated choices and actions, revealing pattern and meaning in the daily swirl.

Then I began to work in an office.

Work, in fiction, belongs to police officers. Also to the "honest toil" of manual labor. Why is office work, a significant part of existence for millions of people in our postindustrial age, so rarely depicted in fiction? Perhaps it's tricky to render the drudgery that characterizes much of it without falling into tedium on the page.

Hazzard noted that an office is "difficult ground for fiction, but nevertheless a human place, made up of human beings." *People in Glass Houses*, the collection of stories arising from her experience of working at the UN, is a scathing and hilarious satire of office life; given the shortfall between the grand aims and petty actuality of "the Organisation," the stories also come within the compass of tragedy.

For Hazzard's generation, the UN represented, first, hope; later, hope squandered. It explains the vehemence of her attack, which would be sustained in her nonfiction books about the UN. A satirist always begins as an idealist. *It could be otherwise*: the ache that fuels critique.

———

Having written *People in Glass Houses*, Hazzard wasn't done with the subject of office life. If a subject preoccupies a writer sufficiently, a single book isn't enough to exhaust it. I think of the First World War continuing to make its presence felt in the novels Pat Barker wrote after her brilliant *Regeneration* trilogy. Something was left over; it insisted on guest appearances in her later books. So it is with office work in Hazzard: it flares up in the passages describing government ministries in *The Transit of Venus* and the administration of colonial Hong Kong in *The Great Fire*.

In *The Bay of Noon*, when Jenny contracts hepatitis, she welcomes the respite from the military office where she works: "When you are ill, you can only be yourself—whereas in an office one is required always to be somewhat false, at least when one is subordinate. The preference for a serious disease over office life struck me." It strikes me, too.

———

In the UN stories, anyone who shows imagination, intelligence, or compassion is swiftly crushed; in the later fiction, those qualities are displayed above all by the women who work in offices. Through marriage, Caro escapes a life of being condescended to by pompous and stupid men—such as Christian, who returns home one day from the Foreign Office to announce ecstatically, "I have been given Africa."

THE BAY OF NOON

The Bay of Noon was the first Hazzard novel I read, and I read it as if bound by a spell. Related in the first person, it offered an immersive narrative, and I succumbed to its claims on my sympathy and attention at once. I was in my twenties, recently back in Australia after living in France. I identified intensely with Hazzard's Jenny, whose private drama was lifted into grandeur by the antique, European background against which it played out.

The greedy, gulping way I read *The Bay of Noon*—a child devouring sweets—returned me to childhood and whole days spent deep in fictional worlds. It was reading as a form of enchantment, a way of reading I continue to value and need. There are novels that, like beloved people, stand between us and the world. They do this by altering our relation to time. They pass through it. They render time irrelevant.

Decades have passed, but whenever I open *The Bay of Noon* a strong magic still comes off the book. When I try to locate its source, I think of the novel's rapturous evocation of Naples. Jenny discovers the city as a young woman, at a period when the self is adult yet porous. Naples offers her expansion and transformation; it reveals her to herself.

When writers describe cities they have known since childhood, the result might be deeply affectionate but it won't be enthralled. Hazzard arrived in Naples in her twenties, and she writes of the city with wonder (of which ignorance is a necessary component). It's the difference between Christina Stead's intimate vision of Sydney and Jessica Anderson's enraptured response, between Elena Ferrante's Naples and Hazzard's. When I experienced *The Bay of Noon* as enchantment I was merely repeating Hazzard/Jenny's entranced encounter with Naples. All of us were young, open to the luster of the world.

It's difficult to write a novel with a first-person narrator who's sympathetic without being dull. The difficulty is one of voice and how to make it sustain interest. If the narrator is blandly congenial, there's a risk of boredom. Nodding and nodding agreement, the reader nods off. An unsympathetic first-person narrator is livelier but just as demanding to maintain; both caricature and a knowing smugness—writer winking across the page at reader—must be fended off.

Jenny is agreeable, ordinary, and spirited, a technical feat in herself.

One way to think about *The Bay of Noon* is as an expert sleight of hand. It draws attention to love: the principal characters fall in love, or fail to do so, or come up against the limits of love, and these entanglements drive the plot. But they have nothing to do with the novel's considerable emotional force. The intimacy charted in layered detail in these pages is a friendship. Jenny and Gioconda become friends and then they betray each other. The delight, the discoveries, the winding conversations, *the enchantment*: it all belongs to them.

There's another hidden-in-plain-view aspect to *The Bay of Noon*. The novel is ostensibly—one might almost say ostentatiously—sumptuous. Folded into it are spectacular things: an ancient city, magnificent architecture, beautiful women, paintings, poetry, the sweep of a fabled bay. The narrative deals in the large, elemental passions set loose by war, love, betrayal, death. It's a novel of grand illusions—no accident that Gianni, Gioconda's lover, is from the world of cinema. But approach it as you might a painting: stand back and look again. Through the dreamy, Whistleresque opulence, a Cubist pentimento of angular configurations appears.

The first comprises Jenny, her brother, Edmund, and his wife, Norah. Told as backstory, it plays no part in the contemporary narrative. Yet this absence animates everything, sets everything in motion. The novel progresses in a series of triangles that substitute for the original, forbidden one. Gioconda, Gianni, Jenny. Jenny, Justin, Gioconda. Justin, Gioconda, Gianni. Gianni, Jenny, Justin. There are shadowy formations in the background, too: Gioconda, her father, her husband. Gianni, Gioconda, her father. Gioconda, Gianni, his wife.

All those initial "j" sounds. What purpose do they serve? Novelists generally dislike risking confusion by giving characters similar names (although: *Wuthering Heights*). Why do it here? I wonder if there's a game— *un gioco*—going on, something that isn't a joke but partakes of both slipperiness and rules. This is a novel in which desire is unstable and shapeshifting; the characters are strongly delineated, individual, but stand in for each other with relative ease. Only the initial, generative threesome remains distinct in the distance. A rule—the prohibition against incest—asserts itself, after which play is unleashed.

Imperialism, its grandeurs and catastrophes, is another shadowy presence in *The Bay of Noon*. Jenny is sent to South Africa as a child, and later makes a home with her brother in Somaliland. Justin has served in Mombasa during the war; Gianni has lived in Eritrea and later shoots a film in Libya. These African place-names summon the corpses of freshly dead empires: the British, the Italian. Behind them, the ghost of the Roman Empire may be glimpsed, in references to the ruins at Tripoli and Ithaca as well as to those in Italy itself. And since Jenny works for NATO, whose base in Naples is organized around the Sixth Fleet, U.S. imperialism is also creepily present in the book.

Hazzard said that she was born into "conscious-
ness" of war. Her father had served in the trenches
during the First World War. As children, the Bell
sisters in *The Transit of Venus* dread the spectacle of
veterans of that war begging in the streets of Sydney. "In the wringing of their hearts, knowledge
had entered." The Second World War brought
its own horrors, culminating in the atom bomb,
which saw the "confused beginning of [Haz-
zard's] pacifism."

As history—the "knowledge" that wrings the
Bell sisters' hearts—entered Hazzard's fiction, it
oxygenated her work. It's the difference between
The Evening of the Holiday and *The Bay of Noon.*
The characters in the latter are the products of
a world recently convulsed by war, their lives
forever imprinted with its journeys, conflicts,
deaths. They're yoked to history, to forces that
exceed the self.

I think that history is the deep subject of
Hazzard's work.

EXCELLENT DOGS

A "lean white dog blotched with black"—the accuracy of "blotched"!—bounds up to stand "gasping and with legs wide." There is a "little curled chrysanthemum of a dog." And a pug who, greeting a long-lost owner, "trod about with ecstatic paws."

"An old chained dog lay in a patch of shade, lolling tongue, swaying tail: a lapped old boat, weathered and tethered in a calm port."

Not forgetting "the hard apple" of a cat's head rubbed on an arm.

THE TRANSIT OF VENUS

I t's said that *The Transit of Venus* took Hazzard twenty-seven drafts. I find it reassuring to learn that those sentences—that novel—didn't simply arrive on the page.

Equally, I'm moved by Hazzard's patient labor; there's humility in assuming that one's writing requires improvement. And I salute her respect for her readers: her desire to present us with the best she could do.

Hazzard had a remarkable feeling for narrative structure: for twisty chronologies, reversals, delays. Look at the way she handles revelations of death: Justin's in *The Bay of Noon*, Adam's in

The Transit of Venus; most famously, Caro's fate. Like Ted's suicide, these endings are communicated incidentally, almost dismissively. In fiction, death—like sex—is often overwrought. But in Hazzard, details are scant or nonexistent. Her revelations are built on concealment, withholding; the risk of florid sentiment is dodged. The moment of disclosure arrives, passes swiftly, is over. The reader is devastated. That's all.

Charlotte Wood remarks on this, likening the end of *The Transit of Venus* to the way we learn of Mrs. Ramsay's death in *To the Lighthouse*. It's an astute comparison, one that prompted me to think about a difference between the two writers. The audacity of Virginia Woolf's maneuver affects not only the reader but also the fragmented narrative—I daresay it affected Woolf herself. No one had done anything like it before her: the gasp is hers as well as ours. In Hazzard's novels, the shock is felt as fully by the reader but is assimilated by the narrative: there's no disruption of form. Woolf pauses, astonished by her boldness, the risk taken and carried off. Hazzard—cool customer—moves on without a backward glance. It's the difference between the high modernist moment and its mid-century iteration; the lesson absorbed.

An email from Josephine Rowe remarks on the way novelists can be attentive to "echoes": "those pantoum-like repetitions, the way they decay or amplify over the course of a life." Echo patterning is abundant in Hazzard's work. It's one reason her novels linger so long in the mind.

Chris Andrews, reading *The Transit of Venus* for the first time, points out an echo I've missed. When the young woman who tried to warm a soldier's missing feet has grown older, she stands at the bedside of her dying husband and touches the outline of his feet before covering them with a blanket. A hundred or so pages separate the two scenes. A further hundred and fifty pages on, by which time the woman is very old and has dementia, she sees a professor on television explain the origin of the phrase "to have cold feet."

I play a game called Impossible to Imagine:

Impossible to imagine a Penelope Fitzgerald character who is evil.

Impossible to imagine a J. M. Coetzee character having fun.

Impossible to imagine a Shirley Hazzard character who needs the lavatory.

In Hazzard's fiction, bodies suffer pain and relish pleasure. She writes about sex and death, about bodies in ecstasy and agony—bodies *in extremis*, in other words. Her vision is intense, fierce, exalted. It sweeps the heights. It has no interest in the everyday mess and materiality of bodies: jagged toenails, sweaty scalps, fleshly oozings and smells. For all the glorious, worldly detail that ballasts Hazzard's work, her concern is ultimately with the metaphysical. Her fiction poses the question asked by all serious art: how should a person live?

In proposing an ethics of living, Hazzard's characters judge: other people, society, themselves. *The Transit of Venus* is the most perfectly realized of these moral dramas: a novel to which judgment and condemnation are central, a *j'accuse* hurled at the Western world. Not coincidentally, it's the most aphoristic of Hazzard's fiction. Judgments in miniature, aphoristic summations, are built into its prose.

The Transit of Venus left Patrick White unimpressed. He wrote to Hazzard: "What I see as your chief lack is exposure to everyday vulgarity and squalor." As Hazzard pointed out in her reply, there's plenty of "everyday vulgarity and squalor" in the novel—the scenes of office life, for one thing. White backpedaled, saying that he was referring to her "charmed existence," the cushioning that comes with wealth. What that has to do with the novel he prudently didn't try to say.

The vision White brought to his fiction encompassed the lavatory as well as the temple and found transcendence in both. So perhaps what really irked him was the absence of bodily squalor in Hazzard's book. Or perhaps it was the scrupulous yardstick Caro applies to life, which sets her apart from "everyday vulgarity." Of Caro, the narrator says, "She would impose her crude belief—that there could be heroism, excellence—on herself and others until they, or she, gave in."

Caro is tremendous. And scary. She has the idealism and intransigence of a heroine from myth. If she didn't make mistakes, she would be insufferable—it would be like living up close to a flame. "Very judgey," would be the verdict today.

In the standards to which they hold others (and themselves), Hazzard's female characters are considered immoderate by those around them: they are "unrealistic," they exaggerate, they make "excessive demands." "She had no sense of proportion ... and wasn't that exactly the thing one looked for in a woman?" asks a man in one of Hazzard's stories. A different female character wishes that she were less exacting— but it's plain that Hazzard disagrees. She favors "excess" of this kind and not only in the ethical sphere. In one of her stories, a young man writes wonderful poetry—wonderful because it doesn't operate within "the bounds of fastidious reticence."

Excess is an aspect of the romantic. That's why the romantic is belittled and feared. Considered in this light, the women who feature in Hazzard's early fiction aren't dated but adamantine, Antigones in their readiness to act outside social constraints. I wonder if I've misunderstood them. Maybe what I've seen as a limiting focus on love is really a determination that cares nothing for public opinion. In its stoniest manifestation it's Rita Xavier in *The Great Fire*, returning to sit at Peter Exley's bedside day after day.

Alternatively, the absence of "vulgarity" that White decried might refer to Hazzard's prose. Throughout her work, her vocabulary and syntax are lucid, formal, high-flown: the language of the bench. Cliché and jargon—the weasel words of commerce and bureaucracy—are satirized, as they are in White, but Hazzard doesn't have the delight in colloquialism and the vernacular that puts the crunch in White's prose.

Another thing: I have a hunch that Hazzard read White attentively while writing *The Transit of Venus*. It's there that she calls Australian history "dun-coloured," dipping her lid to White's notorious complaint about "dun-coloured" realism. The novel also displays several tics characteristic of White's distinctive style and found rarely, if at all, in Hazzard's early fiction:

Intermittent second-person narration: "You could also deliver your opinion, seldom quite favourable, while walking home."

The omission of subject pronouns: "She had of course known [. . .] how leaves fall in deciduous

England. But still been unprepared for anything extreme as autumn."

Transitive verbs used intransitively: "They prowled among chiffoniers and credenzas, and no one had the heart to deny."

Turns of phrase imprinted with White's rhetorical stamp: "Caro was becoming flesh. Her hands were assuming attitudes."

Combinations of these things: "On such a morning you might love the white flowering earth as if you, or it, were soon to die. Left to herself, Caroline Vail might have run through fields or gardens."

(The White imprint will reappear, less strongly, in *The Great Fire*.)

Neither writer might have registered the homage. Yet surely White was attuned to it on some level—he was an excellent reader—and I wonder if it underwrote his reaction to the novel. Imitation might be the sincerest form of flattery but it's rarely the most welcome kind.

———

Don't think I'm letting White—the old monster!—off the hook. "Your chief lack": cruelty in three words. Impossible to imagine having written *The Transit of Venus* and receiving a response like that. From another writer. And not just any writer but Patrick White, Nobel laureate, whose work Hazzard had reviewed with warm intelligence and whom she counted as a friend.

Perhaps White simply missed the point of the novel. It happens. Francis Steegmuller said, "No one should have to read *The Transit of Venus* for the first time." When I read it for the first time, I wondered: Why the fuss? I finished the novel and forgot about it for twenty years.

Then came *Greene on Capri*, Hazzard's memoir about her friendship with Graham Greene. As I slotted it into my bookshelves, my eye fell on *The Transit of Venus*. I took it down and, standing there in my living room, opened the book. The sensation came, like a blow to the breastbone, while I was still on the first page: the shock of the great. I read the novel straight through, with barely a pause. I've returned to it many times, always with a shiver along the nerves.

So what went wrong all those years ago? In the first place, *The Transit of Venus* played havoc with my expectations of Hazzard's fiction. Instead of offering immersion and enchantment, *The Transit of Venus* —set in the drab postwar Anglosphere— encourages detachment and appraisal. It presents itself as spectacle, as Brechtian estrangement. Characters are often referred to by their full name; sometimes they're merely "the man" or "the woman." These cool designations foster observation rather than identification. We watch and assess the characters like people in a painting. This distancing operates even at the level of rhetoric. The narrative is steeped in irony, a trope that promotes seeing through rather than seeing with, a trope associated with disabused, not enchanted, vision.

Notable, too, are the pivotal scenes of observation within the novel (often involving glass). Transfixed, Ted first sees Caro at the top of a flight of stairs, while she looks down at him in turn. Caro and Grace first notice Paul through a window; similarly, Caro and Adam, her future husband, first see each other through a pane of glass. In the most powerful of these frozen observations, Paul's fiancée looks up at a window to see Paul there with Caro naked beside him. At each point, the narrative momentum slows and stills: we stand back and observe the characters observing each other.

Even sympathetic characters are held up to dispassionate scrutiny, like heavenly bodies viewed through a telescope. Ted, the most admirable figure in the novel, remains callously indifferent to his wife. Plain, socially awkward Ted Tice, "the ginger man," is a stubbornly unromantic hero, the antithesis of the tempestuous, darkly handsome Latin male leads in Hazzard's earlier novels; he even has a comic name.

As for Caro, she values "excellence" but falls for a deeply flawed man. Paul Ivory is an *homme fatal* who can trace his ancestry to the likes of sexy, amoral George Wickham and Frank Churchill. Paul, too, will be revealed for what he is, and like Austen's heroines, Caro will see truly and choose correctly at last. But where is the woman whose first pick would be Ted over Paul? The meeting of true minds is a great thing, but sex isn't about the meeting of minds.

Ted Tice: "a callow ginger presence in a cable-stitch cardigan." There are epithets that are fatal to a character. It's possible for a novelist to write against the romantic grain so successfully that when the moment for romance arrives, the reader thinks: Poor Caro. The ginger man opens his arms.

When Charlotte Wood read *The Transit of Venus*, she found herself "confronted and moved and full of a feeling of wanting, somehow, to live up to [the novel], and to Hazzard's demands." We judge Hazzard's characters and, beyond them, the world that has produced them; and beyond that, frighteningly, the novel invites us to judge ourselves. As the narration pulls back again and again from psychology to linger on surfaces and exteriors, our desire for interiority is turned inwards. We're surprised into self-evaluation. In these pages, as in Caro, judgment "perseveres like a pulse."

"Men go through life telling themselves a moment must come when they will show what they're made of. And the moment comes, and they do show. And they spend the rest of their days explaining that it was neither the moment nor the true self."

Is there anyone who reads those sentences and isn't reminded of petty calculations, shabby betrayals, staggering cowardice in matters great and small—in short, the whole shameful accounting that adds up to a life? *I am seen* by the book I'm reading. The sensation is awful. *Oh*

Christ! It is the Inchcape Rock! Not a reaching into the soul but a summons. My soul had been peacefully submerged in everyday blobbiness. Now it stands blinking, called into the light.

They should forbid the paintings to touch you.

There are moments when we recognize our inner selves in novels. It might be why we read them: to feel that we're not floundering alone in the indifferent, midnight murk of the universe, for here is the lifeline of a kindred voice. We are saved, reassured.

Being seen by a book is quite another thing. It means being yanked out of self-love and submitted to scrutiny. The possibility of transformation hovers, and that's always disturbing. Truly, the intimacy of Hazzard's novel is intolerable. It's the narrative counterpart to Rilke's "You must change your life."

No wonder *The Transit of Venus* refused my attempt to read it dreamily, like a child. Its call to reckoning is a matter for adults.

———

Caro and Ted see an amusement park, whose sign "had lost its introductory F, and read, in consequence, UNFAIR." It's one of Hazzard's wry jokes as well as something more: an acknowledgment of the tears of things.

Late in life, Caro realizes that "Even those who have truly lived will die"—a crushing truth. One way to think of *The Transit of Venus* is as an extended gloss on Auden's "We must love one another and die" (famously revised from "We must love one another or die"). Like Auden's revision, Hazzard's novel is unsentimental through and through. It calls for personal integrity, but never mistakes the "flicker of intense and private humanity" for a prophylactic against "the colossal scale of evil" in the world. Evil can only be "matched" by integrity—not prevented.

Adam fights to save South American activists condemned to death. He fails, and keeps vigil with Caro for the men at the hour of their execution. It's an almost unbearable episode: a "matching," useless, necessary, doomed. The best hope is the same bleak one Hazzard outlines in an essay on the nuclear age: that our "history of individual gestures—the proofs of decency, pity, integrity, and independent courage" will make the destruction of the world not "entirely deserved." She might have been remembering Montale's "Little Testament," which puts its faith in "the tenuous spark" of ethical actions as darkness descends on the West.

Graham Greene described Hardy's novels as "desperate acts of rebellion in a lost cause." Hardy haunts *The Transit of Venus* and its fated lives; from the outrageous coincidences in the novel to Christian's sexual exploitation of a young woman in his office, a modern recasting of Alec d'Urberville's pursuit and rejection of Tess. Then there's the sheer inexorability of Hazzard's novel. Starting with the casual announcement of Ted's death in its early pages—possibly the most brilliantly handled instance of foreshadowing in literature—the narrative steadfastly propels its characters towards catastrophe. While entirely harmonious with the governing trope of astronomy (destiny, for these characters, is as immutable as the movements of the stars), the impression of preordained doom is also *echt* Hardy—and who can read Hardy and calmly acquiesce to his iron designs? Why must the vital letter go unread? Why must things invariably take a turn for the worse? I want to shout: *It's not fair!*—the cry that rings through childhood. The funfair turns out to be unfair: it still has the power to make me squirm.

One reason I value *The Transit of Venus* is because it reminds me not to mistake the limits of my understanding for the limits of art.

A GHOST STORY

There are many reasons to read *Greene on Capri*, but for me the book is memorable chiefly for an effect that I can't recover now. It was brought about by the passage in which Hazzard visits the Villa Fersen. Magnificent yet derelict, "inexpressibly romantic in its solitude and decline," the villa is a house from a story or a dream. A sweeping terrace confronts the bay, a haunted drawing room sheds stucco and gold leaf, there's a graceful, breakneck stair. The neglected garden, "encroached on by a cloud of ferns," is a place "of mossy textures and dark dense greens, with impasto of luminous flowers: a place of bird-song and long silence; of green lizards and shad-owy cats and decadent Swinburnean beauty."

The first time I encountered Hazzard's description of the Villa Fersen, a weirdness occurred. I had never been to Capri, never seen an image of that house. *But I knew it.* The picture I carried in my mind was hazy, somewhat bleached. It was lit like a memory but also like a vision. The sea—or the sky—lay off to one side, very flat, very blue.

There's the moment when you see yourself in a book, and the moment when a book sees you. And a third kind, rare, spooky: when something recognized that isn't a memory comes out of a book to find you; it might be something that's waiting to arrive. When time is revealed not as a flow but a tangle. The moment passes. A shimmer is left behind.

THE GREAT FIRE

Hazzard's first three novels end with journeys, but her last begins with one: a man on a train is reading a book. The man who meets him at his destination is reading the same novel. So *The Great Fire*, a double narrative, opens with a journey into a novel and with a doubling.

The pattern will repeat: once again, two men will turn out to be reading the same book. Aldred Leith and Peter Exley have met during the war, but their friendship hasn't ended with it. Continuing into peacetime, theirs is a fellowship of the book and of "quiet speech." A terrible conflict has ended; the world breathes easily once more and reads.

———

The first thing Aldred notices about Helen Driscoll is her hand, which he glimpses down the length of a dining table. "He waited for the other hand to appear, as a watcher of birds awaits the arrival of the mate, the pairing." So Hazzard's last novel links to her first, to Sophie's hand in the fountain catching Tancredi's eye. But this time the social implications of that pretty young hand will not be parsed. It will remain a sign purely of desirable femininity; a little unearthly, like the love affair it triggers, detached from the world.

I don't entirely buy Helen and her brother Benedict's intimacy, the coincidence of their temperaments and tastes. The closeness of these siblings runs counter to the pattern of Hazzard's female protagonists, who typically define themselves against their families. That remains the case even when the relationship is not antagonistic: in *The Transit of Venus*, Caro and Grace are allies yet serve as each other's mirror image, one assertive, the other submissive, and so on; they have "exercised . . . little influence on each other's lives, and exchanged few confidences." But the real contrast with the Driscoll siblings is found in Jenny's love for her brother in *The Bay of Noon*. Where Hazzard presents family intimacy as a source of danger, she sounds convincing and at ease.

Distance brings safety. Jenny, Helen, the Bell sisters: all are expatriates, as was Hazzard herself. She quotes Cyril Connolly to the effect that expatriation is "a desire for simplification." Moving away is a classic solution to the complication called family. It becomes one of the things left behind.

Paying attention is a moral act.

The Great Fire pays quite a lot of attention to Rita Xavier, who belongs to Hong Kong's Portuguese community. "Portuguese," in the context of 1940s Hong Kong and Macau, is a

nineteenth-century British designation indicat-
ing someone of Chinese and European ancestry,
a Eurasian.

As a Sri Lankan Burgher, I pay attention to
the (rare) Eurasian characters I come across in
fiction. Rita is a typist in a British Army office
in Hong Kong. She's a Catholic of good family,
who "holds aloof" from a co-worker who is also
Portuguese. Both "deal brusquely with the Chinese." In other words, Hazzard doesn't treat the
Portuguese community as an undifferentiated
mass, but observes that it has its own nuanced social system, its complexities. It's one of the things
that marks her narrative distance from colonial
disdain for Eurasians—a disdain largely shared,
it should be noted, by the colonized who identify
as racially pure.

Peter, the white Australian who gradually
finds himself attracted to Rita, notes that where
marriage is concerned, "the racial lines were
quietly and implacably drawn." Eurasians em-
body unwelcome proof that these lines have been

sexually breached. An Englishwoman remarks that it's "terrible ... when there are children of mixed race." Hazzard constructs her Eurasian characters in a way that implicitly repudiates that thinking; it is sympathetic, attentive, animated by interest and respect.

In the conventional warped representation, Eurasian women are idle, frivolous, deceitful, and—above all—sexually available. Rita gives the lie to that myth. She's serious-minded and acerbic, wears a cross around her neck, presents a "virginal aspect." The British mock her as "that nun" and "Sister Rita." Her modest occupation —realistically, the only kind a Eurasian woman would be likely to find in the colonial administration— belies a solid education. She speaks several languages, including "excellent, cultivated" English—that last detail in contradistinction to the mockery directed at the English spoken by subject races.

At the same time, Hazzard avoids sentimentalizing or idealizing Rita, thereby sparing her the symbolic flattening that readily befalls people of color in novels written by well-meaning whites. Rita has internalized colonial hierarchies of race. Along with her brusque manner towards the Chinese, she dislikes being heard speaking their language—her Asian ancestry is a source of embarrassment, possibly shame. She's a snob into the bargain. When Peter helps a gravely ill Chinese child living in poverty, she does nothing to assist him. Yet Rita doesn't kowtow to the colonizers either. White characters describe her as "prickly"; she talks back, defends her point of view. She refuses to be grateful for considerations that are taken for granted among whites.

Hazzard's understanding of race relations is shrewd. Commenting on Peter's attitude towards Asians, Rita says, "You intend to be kind. But just—so far," accompanying her remark with a chopping gesture.

So there's white liberalism nailed in two sentences.

Onya, Rita! Onya, Shirl!

I have a particular admiration for the Hong Kong segments of *The Great Fire*, possibly because I first read them as a single long story in *The New Yorker* rather than stitched piecemeal into a novel. Also, I have a stake— novelistic, personal—in literary representations of British colonies in Asia, and Hazzard captures those vanished atmospheres and states of mind with astonishing exactness. Maybe it's not astonishing at all, since she had been familiar with them before they entered her life. In Hong Kong in the late 1940s there could still be found people and situations lifted from the pages of Conrad. Hazzard knew them with what Amit Chaudhuri calls "the intimacy reserved for things one has only ever encountered in books and pictures." Her arrival in the colony, a very young woman steeped in fiction, must have been memorable: reality flowing in to confirm the integrity of imagined worlds. Grainy with detail, marvelously evoked, her depiction of Hong Kong has the intensity and authority that come when literature and life converge. And it has Rita Xavier—a more complex and satisfying creation than Helen Driscoll, to my mind.

Sophie, Jenny, Caro: all have faults— overconfidence in their own judgment, ill-advised desires. Helen is without stain. Perhaps Hazzard thought she was too young to be plausibly flawed, even to the mild degree that her predecessors might be said to err. It wasn't a great move: wholly virtuous characters come at a narrative price.

The Great Fire tells two stories. Helen and Aldred's romance is Peter and Rita's sweetened and writ large. Peter and Rita are secondary, in narrative terms, to Aldred and Helen; they are also more grubbily human. There are obstacles to both affairs: Helen's age, Rita's race. The first problem will be resolved as time passes; the second is insoluble. Peter hesitates to propose marriage as he fears that Rita will suffer under Australia's racial laws. At least that's the public, acceptable face of his hesitation; under it runs his reluctance to leave the safety of *just so far.*

Rita and Peter: their names warn of an outcome that will jangle rather than chime.

Hazzard has said that she fell in love with an older man in Hong Kong, that her mother intervened to part them, and that the relationship didn't survive. In her novelistic revisioning of that experience, Hazzard allows Aldred and Helen the happiness she was denied, while Peter and Rita act out her frustration. I wasn't aware of the autobiographical element when I first read *The Great Fire*, but the secondary story struck me as more forceful than the primary one: partly for the power of its Hong Kong setting, partly because it carries the gritty cogency of unhappiness, partly because it's compressed—one of those distillations of character and situation at which Hazzard excels; most of all because of its relation to history.

In the main strand of the narrative, history

is historical. It's represented by the war, and the war has ended. It has a half-life in the present—the ongoing occupation of Japan and its attendant tragedies—but it plays no determining role in what happens to Helen and Aldred. In love, those two are no larger than themselves. Helen's hand, that dehistoricized sign, is emblematic of their affair. In Hong Kong, by contrast, history is present and oppressive. It manifests itself in opium addiction, in the White Australia policy, in the colonized island itself. It lives in Rita Xavier's DNA. It controls her fate.

Aldred and Helen's share of the novel contains wonderful stretches. As always, Hazzard can't be bettered at conjuring place: Hiroshima after the bomb, London in the aftermath of the Blitz, the end-of-the-world quiet of Wellington. Yet I think of the Hong Kong story as a kernel, bitter and exact. A novel has ripened around it, excellent in parts, elsewhere gone soft.

There are readers who say they aren't convinced that Helen and Aldred would fall in love.

I don't share their view. But I think those readers have sensed the effort that comes with boosting the main narrative: the backstories, the changes of setting, the proliferation of detail and secondary characters—all seductively and expertly rendered, all underwritten by magic. They lend fullness and truth to something that the writer secretly intuits is flimsy (although "secretly intuits" is too cut and dried for this delicate form of knowing). And perhaps "boosting" isn't the word I need for narrative meanderings. Perhaps it's "hesitation." Deborah Levy writes: "A hesitation is not the same as a pause. It is an attempt to defeat [a] wish." Boosting/hesitation happens when a writer's judgment is divided from her wishes. It requires magical thinking. The ending of *The Great Fire* tells us so, for works of art are alive with intelligence about themselves. A hero, whose courage has been tested in battle, travels across the world to a faraway land. The beautiful maiden who has been waiting for him there is asleep; his tears wake her, and then they are in each other's arms. Where does this archetype originate if not in old tales? Wishes have great power in such stories. In *The Great Fire*, I hear Hazzard working to persuade herself that Aldred and Helen's enduring love is more than wishing. But a fulfillment of wishes is what there is at the end.

THE GLITTER

Virginia Woolf believed that fiction should resemble "a spider's web, attached ever so lightly perhaps, but still attached to life at all four corners."

There's much more to a good novel—let alone a great one—than the novelist's powers of observation. But without steady observation of people and the world, fiction lacks energy and conviction. It floats away. One of the admirable features of Hazzard's fiction—and one of the sources of its strength—is its noticing of what is transient and insignificant; its stubborn attachment to life.

Remember the old man hitching his belt?

Here's a waitress clearing a table: "Her stiff,

short skirt spread out around her and exposed the backs of her knees each time she bent over to collect another dish." Here are two friends meeting in a Neapolitan bar: "Standing up at the counter we would have coffee, fierce black coffee, served in tiny cold cups that were always wet from the draining board." Here's a seated man putting away his money: "He put the wallet back into his trouser pocket, stretching out his leg to do so." There's no principle of symbolic equivalence at work in these details. The skirt, the cups, the outstretched leg don't stand for anything. They are themselves, scraps of the world, fully present on the page. What they've come to tell us is straightforward and wonderful: we have been seen.

Poets know the importance of this. "Not ships but one ship with a blue patch in the corner of its sail" for Czesław Miłosz.

Not the grand vague thing but the simple precise one. Not moonlight but the glitter of broken glass.

NOT EXACTLY WHY

hen I look back on half a lifetime of reading Shirley Hazzard, here's what I remember,

The room in which I first read her: a cold Melbourne room, high above a courtyard, in which a green curtain had been drawn back from the window to admit afternoon light. And a different room—dimmer, filled with books—also in Melbourne, in which I began to read *The Transit of Venus* for the second time: the scene of a tremendous revelation.

I remember books that entered my life like events; like meetings with strangers whom one recognizes instinctively as friends.

I remember writing that made a nonsense of time.

I remember writing that proposed a larger life.

I remember writing that expanded my understanding of what it's possible for writing to achieve.

I remember the tribute, compounded of awe and envy, *I wish I'd written that.*

I remember exhilaration. And the rush of gratitude: that such writing existed, that it had come my way.

I remember the lines from Auden that serve as an epigraph to *The Bay of Noon*:

> *though one cannot always*
> *Remember exactly why one has been happy,*
> *There is no forgetting that one was.*

ACKNOWLEDGMENTS

Chris Andrews, Rebecca Bauert, Chris Feik, Sarah Lutyens, Fiona McFarlane, John McGhee, Pat Strachan: *sine qua non.*

Further Reading

BOOKS BY SHIRLEY HAZZARD

NOVELS

The Evening of the Holiday (1966)

The Bay of Noon (1970)

The Transit of Venus (1980)

The Great Fire (2003)

SHORT STORY COLLECTIONS

Cliffs of Fall (1963)

People in Glass Houses (1967)

NONFICTION

Defeat of an Ideal: A Study of the Self-destruction of the United Nations (1973)

Coming of Age in Australia, Boyer Lectures (1985)

Countenance of Truth: The United Nations and the Waldheim Case (1990)

Greene on Capri: A Memoir (2000)

The Ancient Shore: Dispatches from Naples (with Francis Steegmuller; 2008)

We Need Silence to Find Out What We Think: Selected Essays (2016)

INTERVIEWS WITH
SHIRLEY HAZZARD

"Going Against the Grain," *Island* (1992)

"The Art of Fiction No. 185," *The Paris Review* (2005)

"Writing Was Such a Release for Me," *The Times* (2010)

OTHER WORKS CITED

W. H. Auden, "September 1, 1939" and "Goodbye to the Mezzogiorno"

Julian Barnes, "Humph, he, ha," *London Review of Books*

Graham Greene, *The Lost Childhood*

Deborah Levy, *Things I Don't Want to Know*

Czesław Miłosz, "With Trumpets and Zithers"

Eugenio Montale, "Little Testament"

Brigitta Olubas, *Shirley Hazzard: Literary Expatriate and Cosmopolitan Humanist*

Henry Reed, "A Map of Verona"

Rainer Maria Rilke, "Archaic Torso of Apollo"

Susan Sontag, *Against Interpretation*

Patrick White, *Letters*

Charlotte Wood, "Across the Face of the Sun," *Sydney Review of Books*

Virginia Woolf, *A Room of One's Own*

© Mayu Kanamori

MICHELLE DE KRETSER was born in Colombo, Sri Lanka. Her family emigrated to Australia when she was a teenager, and she was educated in Melbourne and Paris. She is the author of five novels, including the Miles Franklin Award winners *Questions of Travel* and *The Life to Come*, the Man Booker Prize long-listed *The Lost Dog*, and a novella, *Springtime*. De Kretser now lives in Sydney with her partner, the poet and translator Chris Andrews. She is an honorary associate of the English depart-ment at the University of Sydney.